CW01151209

Original title:
Tidal Waves of Tenderness

Copyright © 2024 Creative Arts Management OÜ
All rights reserved.

Author: Derek Caldwell
ISBN HARDBACK: 978-9916-90-828-0
ISBN PAPERBACK: 978-9916-90-829-7

Caress of the Cresting Sea

Waves dance lightly on the shore,
Whispers of the ocean's roar.
Foam curls gently in the breeze,
Nature's touch brings quiet ease.

Seagulls soar with graceful might,
Sunset glows in fading light.
Tides embrace the waiting sand,
A soothing touch, a tender hand.

Undercurrents of Love

Deep beneath the surface flow,
Feelings hidden, tides that grow.
Hearts entwined like seaweed cling,
In the silence, lovers sing.

Soft pulses of a silent beat,
In shadows where our spirits meet.
Currents pull, yet hold us tight,
In the darkness, love ignites.

Showers of Kindness

Raindrops fall like gentle hugs,
Nature's tears, like cozy rugs.
Each droplet softens weary hearts,
Kindness flows, it never parts.

Puddles form a shining glass,
Reflecting hope as moments pass.
Tiny gestures, sweet and bright,
Illuminate the darkest night.

Echoes of the Heart's Depths

In the quiet, whispers dwell,
Stories only time can tell.
Echoes linger, soft and clear,
Memories that draw us near.

Every heartbeat, every sigh,
Waves of longing, soaring high.
In the depths, our truths reside,
In echoes, love won't hide.

Waves of Warmth and Understanding

In the stillness, whispers flow,
Each heartbeat sings, a gentle glow.
The ocean's breath, a soothing balm,
Holding all in a quiet calm.

While tides recede, they always return,
Lessons in love, forever we learn.
Guided by stars, we find our way,
In the night's embrace, we softly sway.

Embracing the Soft Sea's Edge

Footprints traced in the golden sand,
Waves decorated by nature's hand.
With every touch, the sea's sweet kiss,
Moments like these, we cannot miss.

Together we stand, the shore on our feet,
Where land and water in harmony meet.
The horizon beckons, a call to explore,
In the heart's language, forever we'll soar.

Flowing Love Beneath the Surface

Beneath the waves, secrets reside,
In depths of emotion, we both confide.
A current strong, it pulls and it sways,
Binding our hearts in mysterious ways.

In the quiet flow, we find our song,
With harmony's rhythm, we can't go wrong.
Ripples of kindness, spreading so wide,
In the sea of love, we shall abide.

Confluence of Kind Hearts

Two rivers meet, a gentle embrace,
Bringing together time and space.
With every drop, a story unfolds,
In unity's warmth, the future beholds.

Through twists and turns, we navigate,
Finding our way, it's never too late.
Hand in hand, on this journey we start,
In the confluence shines the kind heart.

Embracing the Ocean's Serenity

Waves whisper soft secrets,
Underneath a sky so wide.
The sun smiles on the water,
As dreams and waves collide.

Seagulls dance in the breeze,
Echoes of laughter around.
Footprints in the warm sand,
Where the heart's peace is found.

Ripples cradle the moment,
Time stands still in the flow.
In harmony with the tides,
Let the soul's spirit grow.

With every breath of salt air,
Life's worries drift away.
Embracing the vast sea,
Finding calm in the sway.

The Gentle Tide's Lullaby

Beaches hum their sweet song,
With each rise and retreat.
Serenity in rhythm,
Where land and water meet.

Soft crashes on the shore,
Nature's embrace so near.
Every wave a promise,
Whispers only we hear.

Moonlight dances on crests,
As stars twinkle above.
The night holds a lullaby,
Wrapped in ocean's love.

Cradled by the cool night,
I close my weary eyes.
Let the tide sing to me,
In its soothing sighs.

Internal Currents of Warmth

In the depths of my heart,
A river flows with grace.
Warm currents of kindness,
Each ripple finds its place.

Memories like soft echoes,
Cradle me in their glow.
The warmth of shared laughter,
Nurtures seeds that we sow.

Moments weave through the past,
Binding us ever tight.
With love as the anchor,
We sail into the night.

No storm can shake our bond,
No wave can pull us apart.
In these currents of warmth,
We'll always find the heart.

Woven Together by Kind Waters

Streams of life intertwine,
Flowing gentle and free.
In this dance of the water,
We find serenity.

Branches touch the surface,
Reflections paint the sky.
Each drop tells a story,
As time trickles by.

Gathered 'round the rivers,
We share dreams and our fears.
The kindness we find here,
Flows with laughter and tears.

Woven by kind waters,
Together we stand strong.
In this tapestry of life,
We've always belonged.

Whispering Waters of Care

In the quiet brook where lilies sway,
Gentle breezes hum and play.
Soft reflections gleam like light,
Whispers of kindness in the night.

Every ripple tells a tale,
Of love that flows without a fail.
Nurtured by the sun's warm grace,
Peaceful moments we embrace.

Heartbeats under the Surf

Underneath the waves' soft sound,
The pulse of life is ever found.
Each beat a promise, strong and true,
Carried by the ocean's hue.

Hear the surf, it calls our names,
In its rhythm, quiet flames.
Love's cadence, timeless and clear,
A melody for those who hear.

Gentle Waves of Embrace

Waves that roll and softly crest,
Hold us close, we find our rest.
In the dance of sea and shore,
A tender touch, forevermore.

Each swell a promise, every break,
A warm embrace that makes us wake.
Together in this fluid space,
We find our hearts and share our grace.

Flowing Beneath the Stars

Beneath the cosmos, rivers gleam,
Reflecting dreams, a tranquil stream.
Stars above in silent cheer,
Guide the waters, crystal clear.

Every current tells a wish,
Carried forth with each soft swish.
In their flow, our hopes unite,
Shimmering softly in the night.

Sweet Streams of Heartfelt Whisperings

In the meadow where whispers flow,
Hearts entwined in gentle glow.
Dreams are spun on fragrant air,
Love's soft song is found laid bare.

Where secrets dance beneath the trees,
Swiftly carried by the breeze.
Each word spoken, tenderly shared,
In the warmth of love declared.

Mellow Tides of Shared Solace

Like waves that roll on sandy shores,
Our laughter mingles, gently roars.
In quiet moments, peace we find,
In every glance, our hearts aligned.

The hush of night, we breathe as one,
Beneath the stars, our fears undone.
In this embrace of moonlit grace,
Together, we shall find our place.

The Soothing Embrace of Nature's Gift

Among the pines, where shadows play,
The whispers of the earth convey.
In every rustle, a tale unfolds,
Of love and joy that nature holds.

The sunlit paths, where flowers bloom,
Invite us to cast aside gloom.
In the stillness, we hear the call,
Of nature's arms that cradle all.

Gathering the Soft Light of Togetherness

In every corner, love alights,
Binding souls on starry nights.
With hands together, hearts will mend,
In twilight's glow, our spirits blend.

The laughter shared, a soothing balm,
In unity, we find our calm.
Through trials faced, we rise and soar,
In togetherness, we're evermore.

Whispering Shores of Calming Thoughts

Gentle waves kiss the sand,
Soft whispers in the air,
The horizon calls my soul,
Embracing peace everywhere.

Seagulls dance upon the breeze,
Nature's song, so sweetly sung,
In the quiet, I find rest,
Where troubles once were clung.

Sunlight sparkles on the sea,
A tapestry of gold,
In every grain, a promise,
Of tranquility retold.

Each moment flows like water,
Hydrating thoughts anew,
In this place of soothing calm,
The heart learns to break through.

Swells of Nurturing Spirits

Waves arise, a loving tide,
Bringing warmth from deep within,
As the ocean pulses slowly,
Filling souls with peace akin.

Each swell lifts our weary hearts,
With the strength we thought was lost,
In the dance of rising waters,
We discover what it costs.

Nurtured in the ocean's arms,
We find solace from the strife,
In the ebb and flow of love,
We are cradled into life.

Embracing each rising crest,
With courage, we will soar,
In the depths of gentle swells,
Our spirits bloom once more.

Sensing the Rhythm of Kindness

A heartbeat shared with whispers,
Kindness flows like stream and song,
In the cadence of compassion,
We remember where we belong.

Soft glances passed in silence,
A touch that heals the soul,
With each rhythm of goodwill,
We make one another whole.

Echoes of empathy surround,
Cradling every fear,
In the dance of understanding,
Love's light is ever near.

Together in this moment,
We find power in the night,
Sensing rhythms of kindness,
It guides us to the light.

Brook of Cherished Emotions

A brook flows over stones so smooth,
Whispers of secrets softly told,
In its depths, emotions linger,
Washing worries, warm and bold.

Beneath the surface, feelings dance,
Carried by the current's grace,
Every drop a memory shared,
In this tranquil, sacred space.

Leaves float gently on the flow,
Stories drifting in the breeze,
Each ripple tells a tale of love,
As the heart learns to appease.

With each bend and twist it takes,
The brook sings a gentle tune,
Cherished moments find their voice,
Beneath the silvered moon.

Dancing Waves of Warmth

Gentle waves in the sun,
Whispers of the shifting sea,
Each ripple sings a tune,
A melody warm and free.

Laughter dances on the shore,
Children play with pure delight,
Footprints left in golden sand,
As day yields softly to night.

Sunsets spill their golden hue,
Colors blend, a painter's dream,
In this moment, all is calm,
Floating on a blissful stream.

Hearts uplifted in the breeze,
Together feeling nature's grace,
Dancing waves send us afloat,
In this warm, embracing space.

Mellow Ripples of Connection

In the quiet of the lake,
Ripples form where two hearts meet,
Soft reflections in the dark,
A bond made in moments sweet.

Fingers touch upon the shore,
Gentle smiles shared with the night,
Whispers float between us slow,
In the glow of the moonlight.

Each ripple tells a story clear,
Of dreams and promises anew,
As we witness stars align,
Together, we shall journey through.

The calm reflects our shared delight,
In stillness, our spirits soar,
Mellow ripples weave our fate,
In the love that we explore.

Lanterns on the Water's Edge

Lanterns glow with a warm embrace,
A guiding light upon the lake,
Softly drifting with the breeze,
A path for dreams, a chance to wake.

Shadows dance as night descends,
The water shimmers under stars,
Each light a hope, a whispered wish,
Together we mend all our scars.

Colors blend in fragile flames,
Reflections flicker in the night,
We'll find our way through the dark,
With lanterns glowing, hearts in flight.

The world quiets, but our spirits sing,
As stories weave with every glow,
Lanterns on the water's edge,
Guide us where love and kindness flow.

Sway of the Weeping Willows

In the breeze, branches sway low,
Whispering secrets of days gone by,
Weeping willows, graceful and wise,
Watch over lovers as seasons fly.

Their shadows dance upon the ground,
A gentle cradle for hearts entwined,
In soft rustles, sweet promises made,
In their shade, solace we find.

Roots deep set in the earth's embrace,
As time flows gently like a stream,
Underneath, a world so serene,
Together, we nurture our dream.

With every sway, a heart is healed,
In nature's arms, we learn to grow,
Weeping willows, guardians true,
In their kindness, our love will flow.

Delicate Ripples of Love

In the stillness of night,
Whispers dance, soft and light.
Hearts entwined, gently sway,
Guiding dreams on their way.

Shimmering stars above,
Echo the pulse of love.
Each heartbeat, a sweet sound,
In this magic profound.

Secret smiles we trade,
Under the moonlight's shade.
A tender touch, a glance,
In this beautiful trance.

Together, we float free,
In love's sweet symphony.
Delicate ripples play,
As night turns into day.

Underneath the Vast Embrace

Beneath the sky so wide,
Our souls wander side by side.
Every breath, a new start,
In the depths of the heart.

Clouds drift, a gentle art,
Painting dreams, an open chart.
Moments shared, precious gold,
In this tale, we unfold.

Waves crash with soft sighs,
As the sun starts to rise.
Holding tight, never roam,
In your arms, I find home.

Stars fade, but not our light,
Shining ever so bright.
Underneath this vast sea,
Love's embrace carries me.

The Soft Tide of Emotions

Like a whispering breeze,
Emotions rise with such ease.
The tide ebbs and flows,
Carrying all that it knows.

Gentle waves kiss the shore,
Reminding us of the core.
Each feeling, a soft song,
In this world, we belong.

Through storms that may appear,
Faithful hearts will persevere.
A melody of sweet grace,
In this boundless space.

As the moon guides the night,
We find strength in the light.
The soft tide will reveal,
All that is true and real.

Where Kindness Flows Freely

In the heart of the town,
Kindness wears a bright crown.
Gestures simple and small,
Creating warmth for us all.

A helping hand extended,
With love that's never ended.
In every smile shown wide,
Though storms may try to hide.

With every gentle word,
Healing softly is heard.
Unity wraps around,
In this safe, sacred ground.

Where kindness flows like streams,
And nurtures our wild dreams.
Together we will stand tall,
In the love that binds us all.

A Gentle Voyage of Connection

In quiet waters we sail,
Beneath a sky of soft hue,
Whispers of hearts intertwine,
As dreams in silence accrue.

The compass of trust guides us,
Through storms that may arise,
Anchored in hopes unyielding,
We journey toward clear skies.

Each wave tells of stories shared,
Echoes of laughter resound,
In this gentle voyage we take,
A bond that knows no bound.

With every ripple that forms,
Connections are softly spun,
Together we navigate life,
As one, we shine like the sun.

Embracing the Sunset's Glow

The sun dips low in the sky,
Painting the world with gold,
Embracing each fleeting moment,
In warmth as night unfolds.

The horizon whispers secrets,
Of dreams that kiss the sea,
In twilight's gentle embrace,
We find tranquility.

Colors blend in perfect harmony,
As shadows start to play,
We cherish the dusk's blessing,
In twilight's soft ballet.

Together, we watch in silence,
As daylight bids adieu,
In the beauty of the sunset,
Our hearts feel something new.

The Murmurs of Empathetic Souls

In quiet corners we gather,
Where thoughts can softly flow,
Voices rise like gentle rivers,
As understanding starts to grow.

Each whisper holds a lesson,
And every tear is shared,
In the warmth of empathic hearts,
We find how much we cared.

Listening with open spirits,
We weave a tapestry,
Of stories laced with kindness,
In a world that longs to be.

Together we seek solace,
In the murmurs of the night,
As empathetic souls unite,
Their love a guiding light.

Rippling with Compassionate Intent

Ripples spread across the lake,
As kind thoughts take their flight,
Compassionate hearts awaken,
In the glow of shared light.

Intentions bloom like wildflowers,
In a meadow vast and wide,
Nurturing the spirit's essence,
With every gentle stride.

The wind carries whispers of hope,
Strengthening our resolve,
With each ripple of kindness shared,
Our mysteries evolve.

Together we stand united,
In love's most tranquil sea,
Rippling with compassionate intent,
We shape our destiny.

Ebb and Flow of Affectionate Dreams

In twilight's glow, we softly sigh,
Whispers of love drift gently by.
Moonlit paths where shadows meet,
Hearts entwined, so bittersweet.

Waves of laughter in the air,
Moments cherished, beyond compare.
The tides of time forever chase,
Our dreams alight in tender space.

As dawn ascends with golden light,
Love's embrace, a pure delight.
Through every rise and every fall,
In dreams we find our endless call.

Ebbing softly, safe and sound,
In affection, forever bound.
With every sigh, with every gleam,
We'll dance within our shared dream.

The Flowing Heartbeat of Connection

In every glance, a spark ignites,
Silent vows in starry nights.
Two souls merging, softly intertwined,
The flow of love is rare and kind.

Heartbeat's rhythm, steady and true,
Two hearts whispering, just me and you.
Moments fleeting, yet they remain,
In every joy, in every pain.

A bond so deep, it flows like streams,
Carving valleys, shaping dreams.
Each pulse a promise, rich and rare,
In the flow, we find our care.

Connections bloom like flowers bright,
Guiding us through the darkest night.
Together we stand, never apart,
In the flowing pulse of every heart.

Unraveling Layers of Gentle Touch

With fingertips, we trace the skin,
Each layer whispers of where we've been.
A delicate dance, our souls unfold,
In gentle touches, stories told.

Layers peel back, revealing gold,
In every warmth, a world to hold.
Tender moments cascade and flow,
As we discover the depths below.

In quiet hours, soft and sweet,
We navigate where hearts may meet.
In this embrace, we learn and grow,
Unraveling secrets we both know.

Each touch a map, each sigh profound,
In gentle layers, love is found.
Together we weave a tapestry bright,
In the gentle shadows of soft light.

Depths of Compassionate Reflections

In still waters, we gaze within,
Reflecting whispers where love begins.
Compassion flows from heart to heart,
In every glance, a work of art.

Beneath the surface, layers hide,
In tender truths, we confide.
Through storms we weather, hand in hand,
Compassion blooms like grains of sand.

Thoughts intertwine in sacred space,
Each remembrance brings a warm embrace.
Mirrors cast a glow of grace,
In the depths, our fears we face.

Reflections shining, soft and clear,
In every moment, you are near.
Together we dive, love's sweet affection,
Into the depths of our connection.

Pulses of Compassionate Breezes

Whispers of kindness in the air,
Gentle sighs of love everywhere.
Hearts awaken, feeling alive,
In the warmth where hopes thrive.

Laughter dances on the street,
Echoing joy with every beat.
Dreams take flight like birds in spring,
In the breath of life, we sing.

Rainbows shimmer in the sky,
Connecting souls as they pass by.
Unity flows through hands held tight,
Together, we create the light.

With every pulse of the breeze,
Embracing all, we find our peace.
Compassion wraps the world we know,
In every heart, compassion grows.

The Cascade of Soft Emotions

Flowing gently like a stream,
Emotions swirl, like a dream.
Tender feelings rise and fall,
In this dance, we feel it all.

Words like raindrops softly fall,
Nourishing hearts, a loving call.
Hope cascades in colors bright,
Bathing our spirits in warm light.

Moments linger, soft and sweet,
Memories made in each heartbeat.
Gentle touches weave their truth,
In the rhythm of our youth.

Life's sweet currents, they entwine,
Creating stories, yours and mine.
Together, we form a blend,
In this cascade, love will mend.

Rushing Cascades of Empathy

Rushing waters carving through,
Empathy flows, pure and true.
Feeling others' joys and pains,
In our hearts, compassion reigns.

Waves of kindness crash and swell,
In their embrace, we dwell well.
Every heartbeat shares a role,
Binding us, we become whole.

Bridges built on shared despair,
United breaths fill the air.
Gentle whispers stir the soul,
In the rush, we find our goal.

Through the torrents, we will stand,
Linked together, hand in hand.
In this river's swift embrace,
Empathy finds its rightful place.

Serene Floods of Heartfelt Moments

A tranquil tide that softly stirs,
Filling spaces, love occurs.
Heartfelt moments, pure and bright,
Shimmer softly in the light.

Gentle waves of warm embrace,
Cradle dreams in tender grace.
Every heartbeat tells the tale,
In this flood, we shall not fail.

Serenity wraps us tight,
Holding us through day and night.
Moments shared beneath the stars,
Carried softly, near or far.

As the river flows and bends,
In each twist, a love that mends.
Together, we create the song,
In these floods, we all belong.

The Gentle Wave's Embrace

The ocean whispers sweet and low,
Embracing shores where breezes blow.
A rhythm soft, a tender sigh,
As tides unfold beneath the sky.

Each crest a kiss, each trough a dance,
The sea invites a dreamy trance.
With every wave that curls and sways,
It holds our hearts in warm arrays.

In twilight's glow, the waters gleam,
Reflecting all our hopes and dreams.
I find my peace in azure seas,
In gentle waves, my spirit's ease.

Forever held in nature's care,
A haven found, a love laid bare.
The gentle wave, a soft embrace,
Where time dissolves, and we find grace.

Driftwood of Warm Memories

On sandy shores, old driftwood lies,
A testament to time that flies.
Each curve a tale, each knot a thought,
A woven past that love has wrought.

Beneath the sun, a warm embrace,
Each piece a smile, a familiar face.
Connected by the tides of fate,
They carry whispers, though they wait.

Through storms endured and gentle days,
They stand as sentinels of praise.
A memory washed in salty brine,
With echoes of laughter, love divine.

So let us gather years long gone,
In driftwood dreams, our hearts are drawn.
In every grain, a story told,
A treasure chest of warmth and gold.

The Softest Horizon

At dawn, the sky paints dreams anew,
With pastel hues of gentle blue.
Where land and sea, in stillness, meet,
A whispered promise, soft and sweet.

The sun awakes with tender light,
Illuminating paths of flight.
Each wave that breaks upon the shore,
Sings of the love we can adore.

In twilight's glow, we watch in peace,
As day and night, their beauty lease.
The horizon calls with vibrant hues,
Inviting hearts to share their views.

So let us wander, hand in hand,
Across this softly painted land.
With every step, we'll chase the sun,
Together, where our souls are one.

Undercurrents of Loyalty and Love

Beneath the surface, currents flow,
A hidden strength, a steady glow.
With every swell, our hearts align,
In depths where trust and hopes entwine.

The ocean's pulse, a steadfast beat,
In loyalty, we find our seat.
With every wave that rolls ashore,
Our bond grows deeper, more and more.

Through storms that rage and skies that gray,
We navigate the wildest way.
United still, through thick and thin,
The depths of love, we dive within.

So let the world around us change,
Our hearts remain, forever strange.
In undercurrents, strong and free,
Loyalty's embrace, just you and me.

The Sanctuary of Gentle Oceans

Beneath the sky, a peaceful hue,
Where whispers dance, and dreams come true.
The softness of the tide rolls near,
A sanctuary of calm, so clear.

Fingers trace the smooth, wet sand,
Cradled by the sea's gentle hand.
Colors blend at dusk's soft call,
In this haven, I feel small.

The horizon meets the endless blue,
With every wave, I start anew.
A world where worries cease to roam,
In the oceans, I find home.

Flowing Hearts in Harmony

Two souls entwined, a dance begins,
Like rivers flowing, love always wins.
A melody sweet, a song of two,
Hearts in rhythm, forever true.

Beneath the stars, our laughter rings,
In the warmth of love, the heart sings.
Gentle whispers in the night,
Guiding us through soft, dim light.

In every pulse, a promise made,
As long as the sun fades to shade.
Together we journey, hand in hand,
In harmony, forever we stand.

The Serene Embrace of Waves

Ocean's arms wrap me tight,
In each wave, I find delight.
Soft caresses, a soothing balm,
In the tide, I feel so calm.

A quiet space where worries wash,
With each crest, a gentle squosh.
Endless rhythms, the sea's sweet breath,
In this serenity, I find depth.

The sun dips low, the sky aglow,
With every ebb, my spirit flows.
The world dims down, yet I feel bright,
In waves' embrace, all feels right.

Heartstrings Intertwined

In the silence, our hearts connect,
A bond so deep, we can't neglect.
Threads of love, a tapestry,
Woven carefully, you and me.

Each moment shared, each glance we steal,
Unspoken truths in the way we feel.
Gentle touches, a spark ignites,
Two souls merging in starry nights.

Guided by love's endless light,
We navigate through day and night.
Together always, come what may,
In our heartstrings, forever stay.

Undercurrents of Serenity

In whispers soft the waters flow,
Beneath the calm, where silence grows.
A dance of light in shadows deep,
In tranquil depths, the heart can leap.

With gentle tides that ebb and wane,
Releasing burdens, easing pain.
The world turns slow, with peace begun,
As sunset kisses the horizon.

In quiet corners of the mind,
A sanctuary, solace finds.
The ripples speak in soothing tones,
In every heart, a place called home.

So dive within the still blue sea,
Where undisturbed, the heart flies free.
In currents soft, our spirits soar,
Embracing all, forevermore.

Radiant Hues of Compassion

In every smile, a spark ignites,
Colors burst in endless sights.
With every tear, a story shared,
A tapestry of love declared.

The vibrant shades of kindness blend,
In quiet moments, hearts can mend.
Each gesture warm, a touch divine,
Creating bonds that intertwine.

Through gentle words, the heart can heal,
A bridge of trust, a soft appeal.
With radiant hues, we paint the world,
In every soul, compassion swirled.

Together we rise, hand in hand,
In this bright, united land.
Each life a canvas, love defined,
In hues of compassion, intertwined.

The Fluidity of Soft Embrace

In every hug, a warmth unfolds,
A sanctuary from the cold.
As bodies meet, the walls fall down,
In tender folds, we lose the frown.

With every squeeze, a heartbeat's song,
A rhythm shared where we belong.
The fluid dance of breath and sigh,
In moments close, we feel the high.

Through softest touch, the worries fade,
In gentle arms, the price is paid.
A comfort found in shared repose,
In whispered dreams, a love that grows.

So let us weave this thread of grace,
In every corner, our embrace.
The fluidity of love displayed,
In every heartbeat, memories made.

A Voyage Through Warm Waters

In tranquil seas, the journey starts,
With every wave, we share our hearts.
The sun above, a golden ray,
Guiding ships along the way.

Each ripple tells of stories bold,
Of adventures shared and dreams retold.
Together we sail, we laugh, we glide,
In warm embraces, side by side.

The currents pull, but hope's our sail,
As we navigate through every gale.
The horizon calls, with open arms,
In salty air, we find our charms.

So raise your sails to skies so clear,
A voyage grand, without a fear.
Through warm waters, our journey flows,
In every heart, the adventure grows.

Flowing Together in Quietude

In whispers soft, the river glides,
A tranquil path where silence bides.
Each ripple tells a story true,
Of moments shared, both me and you.

Beneath the shade of swaying trees,
We find our peace, a gentle breeze.
The world outside, a distant hum,
In quietude, our souls become.

With each heartbeat, time stands still,
While nature's pulse, our hearts will fill.
Flowing like the water's song,
Together here, where we belong.

In twilight's grasp, the light does fade,
But in this calm, no need for trade.
For in our silence, love's embrace,
Together flow, in sacred space.

Embracing Beneath the Stars

Underneath the endless night,
We find our dreams in soft starlight.
With every twinkle, wishes soar,
An ancient dance, forevermore.

The moon above in silken glow,
Whispers secrets only we know.
In the hush of this serene land,
Two souls entwine, so hand in hand.

Each star a spark of hope and grace,
Illuminating love's warm face.
In cosmic wonder, we reside,
Together, hearts forever tied.

Beneath the velvet, vast expanse,
We surrender to love's sweet chance.
In this moment, nothing wrong,
Embracing dreams where we belong.

Canvas of Kindness Across the Sea

Waves murmur tales of distant shores,
Where kindness flows and love restores.
A canvas painted rich and deep,
With every brushstroke, memories keep.

Across the sea, the heart extends,
In simple deeds, our spirit mends.
With every grain of golden sand,
We weave connections, hand in hand.

The colors blend, a masterpiece,
In unity, we find our peace.
For in the tides, our hearts shall meet,
A harmony where hope is sweet.

Together, threads of kindness spun,
In every smile, we become one.
Across the sea, this bond will gleam,
A canvas bright, a shared dream.

The Gentle Brew of Affection

In morning light, the kettle hums,
A gentle brew that warmth becomes.
With every sip, a moment shared,
In simple joys, our hearts are bared.

The rich aroma fills the air,
Each drop infused with love and care.
As flavors mingle, time stands still,
In this embrace, we find our will.

With laughter mingling like a song,
Together, we know where we belong.
Through quiet chats and whispered dreams,
Our bond grows strong, or so it seems.

As night descends, the mugs held tight,
In every glance, a spark of light.
The gentle brew of pure affection,
Steeps deep within, a sweet connection.

Glimmering Grace on Water's Edge

The sun dips low, a golden hue,
Waves whisper soft, a tranquil view.
Footprints left in the cool, damp sand,
A moment cherished, simple and grand.

Seagulls dance on the evening breeze,
Nature's song, a heart that sees.
Reflections shimmer, a fleeting glance,
In twilight's embrace, we dare to dance.

Horizon of Hushed Hopes

Beyond the waves, where dreams align,
A promise waits on the edge of time.
Softly it calls, like the tide's own sigh,
A beacon bright in a sprawling sky.

Gentle whispers of the night unfold,
Each star a story, a vision untold.
In stillness found where the world takes pause,
Hope takes root, a silent cause.

Map of the Breaking Surf

Lines drawn soft on the ocean's face,
Each crest and trough, a mapped embrace.
Foam-tipped waves reveal the way,
Guiding lost souls, come what may.

Journey forward, amidst the roar,
Adventures await on the distant shore.
Anchored dreams stir with each swell,
Secrets of the sea, in whispers, they tell.

Quietude in the Currents

Amidst the rush, a calm prevails,
Nature's heartbeat sings in details.
Rippling waters, a soothing touch,
In the quietude, we find so much.

Stillness cradles the moment's grace,
A gentle flow, time's soft embrace.
In every ripple, peace takes flight,
As currents carry the day to night.

Dance of the Gentle Waters

Ripples weave through twilight's grace,
Soft reflections in a tranquil space.
Whispers of the night unfold,
As water glitters, pure and bold.

Moonbeams waltz on liquid trails,
Casting magic where hope prevails.
Nature's rhythm, sweet and light,
A serenade to end the night.

Gentle breezes join the tune,
Lullabies beneath the moon.
Each drop a story, calm and wise,
Where peace and beauty intertwine.

Dance we shall with every flow,
Heartbeats pulsing, soft and slow.
In this moment, we find release,
A harmony that never ceased.

The Ocean's Cradle of Care

In the arms of waves we find,
A soothing touch, a peace of mind.
The ocean hums a lullaby,
Holding dreams as seabirds fly.

Salt-kissed air, a gentle sigh,
Whispers carried, low and high.
Each crest and trough, a hand of grace,
Nurturing life in every space.

Beneath the surface, treasures lie,
Hopes and fears that dare to fly.
With every tide, a chance to heal,
In the cradle, love is real.

Waves embrace both joy and sorrow,
Reminding us of bright tomorrow.
In each ebb and flow we find,
The ocean's care, forever kind.

Shimmering Streams of Tender Spirits

In the glade where waters gleam,
Whispers of a thousand dreams.
Each stream a pathway, soft and clear,
Guiding hearts to gather near.

Dancing lightly, sunlight plays,
On shimmering hues of gentle rays.
Nature's heart beats strong and free,
In streams that flow eternally.

Waves of laughter, whispers soft,
Carry hopes aloft, aloft.
Tender spirits shape the way,
Through the calm of every day.

In every ripple, stories weave,
Tales of joy that we believe.
With every glance, a world anew,
In these streams, our spirits grew.

Currents of Comfort and Solace

Calm the world with gentle tides,
Where in still waters, peace abides.
Currents wrap like arms of care,
Holding close the dreams we share.

Each wave a whisper, soft and brief,
Washing over wounds of grief.
Time slows down within this flow,
Moments linger, soft and slow.

In currents deep, we dive and soar,
Finding solace at the core.
Hearts united, spirits soar,
In nature's arms forevermore.

Rippling softly, love cascades,
Through darkened nights and dawns that fade.
In the safety of these streams,
We live our lives and chase our dreams.

Beyond the Surface of Understanding

In depths where shadows softly play,
Wisdom whispers through the fray.
Questions linger, minds engaged,
Seeking truths on every page.

The heartbeats echo, pulse of time,
In silence, every thought will rhyme.
Layers deep, the soul unveils,
Stories woven, rich as tales.

Beneath the surface, currents flow,
The unseen bonds that help us grow.
We reach for stars, yet ground our feet,
In every storm, we find our beat.

So let the journey lead us forth,
To corners dark, and places worth.
For understanding blooms in light,
When shadows dance, it feels so right.

Soft Ripples Beneath the Stars

The night unfolds with gentle grace,
Whispers of dreams in a sacred space.
Stars above in velvet skies,
Reflect the hopes in lovers' eyes.

Ripples dance on waters deep,
Carrying secrets that we keep.
A serenade of nature's song,
Where hearts entwine, they belong.

Beneath the moon, where lovers tread,
Soft reflections of words unsaid.
In tranquil moments, time stands still,
As night embraces, quiet and chill.

With every wave, our souls align,
Under the heavens, pure and divine.
Together we'll drift, side by side,
In this cosmic dream, our spirits glide.

Winds of Kindred Spirits

A gentle breeze through open fields,
Brings tales of love that fate reveals.
Kindred hearts, entwined in flight,
Dancing softly in the night.

The winds carry laughter and sighs,
Echoing truth beneath bright skies.
In every gust, a story spins,
Of timeless bonds, where life begins.

Carried off to realms unknown,
Together, never more alone.
With every whisper in the air,
We feel the presence, always there.

So let the winds of spirit soar,
And guide us to forevermore.
In unity, we brave the storm,
Together, with love, we're warm.

The Gardens of Serene Love

In gardens lush, where blossoms bloom,
Love grows softly, dispelling gloom.
Petals whisper secrets shared,
In every glance, two souls declared.

Among the trees, their shadows play,
A tapestry of light and sway.
With gentle hands, they nurture dreams,
In tranquil air, their laughter beams.

Each fragrant breath, a promise made,
In sacred spaces, hearts won't fade.
Hand in hand, through trials they wander,
In nature's grace, they pause and ponder.

For in this garden, love's embrace,
Time stands still, a sacred space.
Together, they shall always grow,
In the warmth of love's soft glow.

Softness Between the Shores

The waves brush lightly upon the sand,
Whispers of secrets from sea to land.
With each ebb and flow, a dance unfolds,
Stories of love that the ocean holds.

Glistening grains in the golden light,
Kissed by the tide, a perfect sight.
Seagulls call out with a joyful glee,
In this soft haven, we roam wild and free.

Breezes bring laughter, soft as a sigh,
Carrying dreams as the clouds drift by.
Moments shared where time seems to pause,
Nature's embrace, our hearts' gentle cause.

Here lies the peace of the world we crave,
In the softness between the shores, we wave.
Let the ocean's melody guide our way,
In this tranquil lull, forever we stay.

Embracing the Whispering Currents

Under the moon's gaze, the waters gleam,
Currents weave tales like a flowing dream.
The night air shimmers with soft-spoken vows,
As stars above watch, with quiet brows.

Each wave a pulse, rhythmic and true,
Embracing the shore with the night's cool dew.
A serenade sings in the hush of the tide,
A gentle reminder that love won't hide.

Echoes of laughter ride on the spray,
Reflections of hearts that dance and sway.
In the whispering currents, our spirits align,
A bond unbroken, a treasure divine.

Holding you close, as the world drifts away,
In this tranquil moment, forever we'll stay.
Embracing the night with hearts all aglow,
In the whispering depths, our love will flow.

Gentle Surge of Affection

Through the twilight mist, the waves kiss the shore,
A gentle surge of affection, forevermore.
Each rise and fall brings a tender embrace,
In the ocean's rhythm, we find our place.

Soft breezes carry the scent of the sea,
A balm for the soul, setting our spirits free.
Moonlight dances on waves, a silvery hue,
With each heartbeat shared, I long for you.

The tides may shift, but my heart stays true,
In the ebbing light, it's always you.
Wander with me, where the ocean meets sky,
In this soft space, our dreams can fly.

Together we'll roam, as the stars guide our way,
In the gentle surge, our hearts will play.
Boundless affection like a whispering tide,
In this sweet moment, let love be our guide.

Caress of the Unseen Ocean

The ocean's caress, soft and unseen,
Wraps around hearts in a silken sheen.
With each gentle wave, a touch divine,
Caressing our souls, forever entwined.

Whispers of waves that cradle the night,
Murmurs of love in the moon's soft light.
Under the sky where the sea meets the land,
We find each other, a perfect strand.

Sailing on dreams, like boats in the blue,
Each breath of salt air brings visions of you.
In the embrace of the night's calm embrace,
We navigate love in this sacred space.

With laughter and light, we drift ever near,
In the caress of the ocean, there's nothing to fear.
Let the tides guide us as we softly sway,
In the unseen depths, forever we'll stay.

The Stillness Between Waves

A hush unfolds upon the sea,
Where whispers dance in harmony.
The water glistens like a dream,
In silence, nature's softest theme.

Each breath, a gentle sigh of night,
As stars begin to twinkle bright.
The moon, a watcher from above,
Cradles the world in quiet love.

The ebb and flow, a soothing tune,
Beneath the gaze of silver moon.
In stillness, time begins to fade,
In tranquil calm, our fears are laid.

The ocean's pause, a tender grace,
Inviting peace in this vast space.
In every ripple, life concealed,\nThe stillness speaks, its truth revealed.

Mirrored Hearts Under Waves

In waters deep, our souls collide,
Reflections dance, no need to hide.
Two hearts entwined in ocean's flow,
An endless bond, where love can grow.

We delve beneath the sapphire tides,
Where secrets dwell and hope abides.
Each wave a pulse, a steady beat,
In depths unknown, our dreams repeat.

The currents pull, yet here we stand,
Together strong, we take a hand.
Mirrored visions in the deep,
Forever ours, our love to keep.

Through every storm, through every calm,
Our spirits soar, a sacred balm.
In unity, beneath the skies,
Mirrored hearts where true love lies.

Embracing the Shore's Gentle Call

The shore beckons with a warm embrace,
Soft sand beneath, a tranquil space.
Waves whisper secrets to the land,
A timeless bond, forever planned.

With every tide, a story told,
In sunlit hues of blue and gold.
The ocean sighs, a soothing balm,
A lover's touch, serene and calm.

Seagulls dance and dive with grace,
As time unfolds, a sweetened pace.
In salty air, our spirits soar,
Embracing the shore forevermore.

With every step, the sea does yield,
The treasures hidden in the field.
We walk as one, hand in hand,
In harmony with sea and sand.

Echoes of Loving Currents

In whispers soft, the night does sigh,
Loving currents weave their cry,
Hearts entwined in shadows cast,
Memories hold, forever last.

Beneath the stars, our dreams take flight,
Flowing rivers, pure and bright,
Every glance, a spark ignites,
Echoes call through velvet nights.

With each tide, our love will swell,
Stories told by the ocean's bell,
Together we dance on silver sands,
Echoing life, hand in hand.

In the silence, find our song,
Where the waves of love belong,
Each heartbeat, a gentle press,
Embraced within our endlessness.

Arches of Soft Light and Love

Beneath the arches, shadows fade,
Soft light glimmers, serenade,
Whispers carry on the breeze,
A tapestry of promised ease.

Through the blossoms, lovers roam,
Finding in each other home,
Gentle hands and radiant eyes,
Crafting dreams beneath the skies.

Fleeting moments stitched in gold,
Tales of warmth and secrets told,
With every laugh, a spark is born,
In twilight's hue, our hearts adorn.

Together wrapped in tender hues,
An embrace of timeless views,
Love's soft light, a guiding star,
In every breath, we heal each scar.

Serenade of the Calming Seas

Waves that whisper, tales of old,
Serenades in breezes bold,
Dance upon the ocean's crest,
Find your peace, your heart's sweet rest.

Moonlit nights, a tranquil song,
In the calm, we both belong,
Voices melding with the tide,
In the depths, love's truth won't hide.

Shores of dreams where wishes play,
Each embrace, a soft ballet,
Alone together, souls set free,
In the tranquil serenade of sea.

Time stands still as waves caress,
A gentle flow, our hearts confess,
Forever caught in ocean's sea,
Gentle tides, just you and me.

Embrace of the Celestial Shores

On celestial shores where starlight beams,
Our love flows through the cosmic dreams,
Every heartbeat, the universe sings,
In the quiet, our spirit clings.

With each touch, the heavens greet,
In constellations, our souls meet,
Galaxies birth in loving grace,
Together we weave through time and space.

The sands aglow with the moon's sweet kiss,
In your arms, I find my bliss,
A universe wrapped in golden weave,
In the dusk, our hearts believe.

Stars align as we softly glide,
Hand in hand, a cosmic ride,
On celestial shores, forever free,
In the embrace of love's decree.

Currents of Compassion

In gentle waves, we find our way,
Hearts united, come what may.
With kindness flowing, hand in hand,
Together, we will understand.

Through trials faced, our spirits grow,
In tender light, our love will show.
Each tear that falls, a lesson learned,
In every heart, compassion burned.

So let us weave a tapestry,
Of hope and joy, of unity.
Where every soul can feel the grace,
Of love's embrace in time and space.

In currents deep, we're never lost,
For with each wave, we share the cost.
Compassion's call, a guiding star,
Together, we can go so far.

Embrace Beneath the Moon

Beneath the glow of silver light,
We hold each other, hearts take flight.
A whisper soft, a gentle sigh,
In night's embrace, together, we lie.

The world fades out, it's just us two,
In this moment, love feels new.
With every glance, our souls combine,
A cosmic dance where spirits shine.

Stars above, they twinkle bright,
Guiding dreams through endless night.
In this stillness, fears subside,
In your arms, I will abide.

As moonlight bathes the earth in peace,
Our bond grows strong, shall never cease.
With every heartbeat, love will bloom,
In this embrace, beneath the moon.

Ocean of Affection

Waves of love crash on the shore,
With every swell, I want you more.
A tide that pulls, a current strong,
In ocean's depths, we both belong.

In every ripple, whispers call,
An endless dance, we rise and fall.
Hand in hand, we face the sea,
In your embrace, I am free.

The salty breeze, a sweet caress,
In this ocean, I find my rest.
With every dawn, a chance to start,
You are the wave that swells my heart.

As sunsets paint the sky with gold,
In ocean's arms, we'll never grow old.
With every heartbeat, love's reflection,
In this vast world, an ocean of affection.

Soft Swells of Serenity

In quiet moments, stillness reigns,
Soft swells carry away our pains.
With gentle whispers, nature sighs,
In perfect peace, our spirits rise.

The world around, a tranquil song,
In harmony, where we belong.
With every breath, we find our flow,
In soft swells, our love will grow.

The sun dips low, the stars ignite,
Wrapped in warmth, we greet the night.
In every heartbeat, calm resides,
In your embrace, my soul confides.

As moonbeams dance upon the sea,
In soft swells, just you and me.
Together as the night unfolds,
In serenity, our love enfolds.

Nestled in the Ocean's Lap

Cradled deep in azure waves,
A world of whispers safely braves.
The tides embrace with gentle grace,
In quiet depths, we find our place.

Coral gardens spread like dreams,
Where sunlight dances, softly gleams.
In currents soft, the secrets flow,
The ocean's heart, a calming glow.

Creatures glide through sapphire light,
In tranquil realms, they take their flight.
The salty air, a sweet caress,
In nature's lap, we find our rest.

With every wave, a story sways,
Of ancient mariners' lost days.
Nestled safe, we hold our breath,
In the ocean's lap, we dance with death.

Sailing Through Sighs

A ship of dreams on rippling seas,
With sails that flutter in the breeze.
Through whispers soft and gentle cries,
We chart our course, all doubts defies.

The moonlight guides our wandering eyes,
As we set sail through silent sighs.
Each wave a tale, a heart's delight,
In tranquil waters, love takes flight.

The stars above, our only guide,
Through stormy nights, a faithful ride.
With every turn, a chance to find,
New shores of peace, with hearts aligned.

Together on this timeless quest,
In oceans vast, we seek the best.
As dawn awakes, with colors bright,
We sail through sighs into the light.

Beneath the Surface of Solace

In quiet depths where shadows play,
Beneath the waves, we drift away.
A sanctuary, calm and deep,
Where secrets of the ocean seep.

Soft currents whisper to our souls,
As peace unfurls and gently rolls.
In blue embrace, we're washed anew,
Beneath the surface, dreams come true.

Each bubble bursts with laughter's song,
In depths where we both still belong.
With every breath, we feel the grace,
Of solace found in this embrace.

Together here, let worries fade,
In harmony, our hearts are laid.
Beneath the surface, life awakes,
In solace deep, love never breaks.

The Salt of Shared Stories

On distant shores where tides collide,
The salt of stories is our guide.
With every wave, a tale unfolds,
Of whispered dreams and hearts so bold.

In salty air, our laughter blends,
As memories weave and never ends.
Each grain of sand, a moment shared,
In ocean's arms, we've always dared.

In circles drawn by firelight's glow,
We gather 'round, let the tales flow.
The salt of life, both sweet and brine,
In every story, your hand in mine.

Through storms and calms, we stand as one,
The tapestry of life's begun.
With every tide, our hearts explore,
The salt of shared stories, forevermore.

Milton Keynes UK
Ingram Content Group UK Ltd.
UKHW021951151124
451186UK00007B/187